Powerhouse Publishing Inc.

ISBN: 978-1-7335157-0-2

Table of Contents

Success Shield

How To Protect Your Mind, Career and Destiny Using Proven Leadership Strategies

Joanna de Peña, M.Ed.

Success is Possible.

Acknowledgements

Altagracia de Pena, Mother

Rafael de Pena, Father, RIP

Jenny Alvarez, Best Friend

Dr. Lindsay, Mentor, RIP

Steve Kelley, Mentor

This has been one of the most rewarding experiences I have had. Writing this book has been a challenge, and a blessing in disguise. This book is a tool to break barriers within our upcoming generations. None of this would have been possible without my support system that cheers me on, even if they don't understand how I will get it done.

To my mother, who has been my biggest cheerleader in all of my endeavors, she always listened when I had my initial ideas for this book. She always provided a sense of the sky is not the limit, and always encouraged me chase my desire to write. I am forever grateful for her positivity, love, and unconditional support. Do you know how it feels when someone truly believes in you? I do because of her, thank you mom.

To my father, thank you for teaching me the value of mastering anything I do. Because of you, I am competitive, hardworking, and compassionate. Although you got sick when I was 9, I always saw your joy when I visited you at the nursing home, especially when I came in with my graduation gown and diplomas. I will never forget the expression on your face when I told you I studied in Costa Rica, Spain, and France in high school. I never thought I would write a book and I wish you were here to read it, I know you are in heaven smiling. Thank you. Rest in peace.

I'm eternally grateful of my best friend and business partner, Jenny. Together we are a powerhouse force. There are no words to describe my deep appreciation for you and your willingness to drop anything to be there for me. You are someone that I truly appreciate. Whatever business decision I decide to do, you are the first one to say, "Ok, let's do it." Thank you for staying up countless days until 3am at times to listen to me read my book out loud when I needed it. Your dedication to my success means the world to me.

To my dearest mentor, Dr. Richard Lindsay. Thank you for believing and supporting me since I was a high school senior. You have inspired me to chase my dream, even if I don't have all the answers. This book was just that! I learned that anything is possible, even if it seems foreign at first. Because of people like you, who genuinely cared and believed, I did it. This book was inspired by my organization, Top Notch Scholars, and Top Notch Scholars is alive because of you. Thank you for your mentorship and life guidance, I know you are still on my team, although you are in heaven. May you rest in peace.

To Steve Kelly who dedicated time to me when I was 9 years old and developed me into a "beast" (great) basketball player; hard work truly does pay off. Thank you for pushing me and always guiding me in the right direction. I have developed a mentality that never gives up and because of you I never give less than 100% in anything I do. Your mentorship brought me to places, countries, and experiences I never thought possible growing up in an inner city. I thank you for instilling values, building my character through sports, and lending an ear when I needed it.

FOREWORD

Raisa T. Carrasco-Velez

I am a youth development professional who entered the field while still a teenager. The time period was challenging but magical. It was the late 80s and I, like thousands of young immigrants, landed in one of the most vibrant gateway cities in the United States: Lawrence, Massachusetts. At the time, the city had the highest teen pregnancy rate in the state and as a young professional I was both intrigued and troubled by the data.

I accepted my first job offer as a youth health educator and outreach specialist at an agency serving newly arrived immigrants and refugees. I found myself intentionally collaborating with youth-serving agencies and doing outreach anywhere young people frequented—parks, churches, schools, and at a place known as the beacon of hope the Boys & Girls Club of Lawrence.

At the club I had an opportunity of a lifetime. I became a director and enjoyed the one-to-one time I needed to understand and learn the realities lived by the children I served. There I met Joanna DePena and our journey began. Her energy, enthusiasm, and genuine smile automatically captured my heart. Every young person I met had aspirations, but Joanna had a plan. She was eager to experience all life had to offer. I was one of several mentors and caring adults who joined her and supported her while she explored opportunities.

Despite the obstacles Joanna encountered in middle school, she pushed through and secured a full-tuition scholarship at a prestigious prep school. Her new environment offered high-quality education and more. I still treasure the gift she brought me from her first trip abroad, a replica of the London clock tower, a place I have yet to visit!

Life has unique ways of setting the stage for great things to come about. Our paths crossed again one summer night when Joanna sat in my class as a graduate student pursuing a master's degree. Back then JoJo, the young ball player with a killer smile who remained full of dreams, was my student, and today I am proud to call her my colleague. Joanna has written this wonderful book to shine the light and to rewrite the narrative for youth.

Success Shield reflects Joanna's passion, vision, and strategy. It's an invitation to embrace leadership and to own one's life outcomes. At a time when lack of leadership and integrity threaten the future of all youth, particularly those in marginalized communities, this book is a much-needed read.

I am honored to be a witness and active participant in Joanna's life. I invite the reader to discover through Joanna's never-ending passion and sincere work, a path to living a purposeful life and positively impacting social change. May you find lifelong mentors, face challenges with passion, lead with love, and above all stay true to your voice.

Chapter 1

A Message To The Reader

I am so happy that you are about to embark in this new journey. The journey to become the best version of yourself. I am so proud of you! Many people say that they want success, but very few do anything about it. I am excited to share with you the very mindset that keeps me pushing forward day in and day out regardless of the negativity I may come across, the daily failures, how exhausted I may feel, and the number of doors that may close on me. It is not about how many doors of opportunity close on you, it is about how many doors you choose to continue to knock on. This game of life is beautiful; be optimistic, be grateful and be of service to others.

By being optimistic, we let go of any fears that may be holding us back from our next big opportunity. Get EXCITED about your future, it's yours, and you only have ONE life to live. Life is not easy, but if you understand that every day is an opportunity for your growth then you will give 100% of your time and energy towards your future. If you give anything less than 100% you will miss opportunities of ideas, solutions, and connections that can catapult you to the next step in your life.

By being grateful, we become humble. Life is not a race and we should not be measuring our successes against our peers because we are all on a different life path pursuing different passions. Take a moment and look around you, look at yourself in the mirror, look at what you have accomplished, and look at what you will be accomplishing very soon. You are lucky, you are blessed, you are destined for greatness. Remain humble and stay focused because when times get tough you will need the mental ability to think clearly, analyze your obstacles, and effectively reach out to those who may be able to lend an ear and provide wisdom and direction. This cannot happen if you are distressed or blocking people out of your life.

I am a firm believer that while we are on this journey toward personal success, we should serve others as much as possible. You may read that and think, "Joanna, I need to work, study, pay bills, and focus on me." These are all valid responsibilities; however, if you look at the bigger picture you will quickly realize that even the very jobs you take on serve people in one way or another. Whether you are a cashier at McDonald's or a financial analyst at a big corporation, you are serving people. We should also give back. Whether that be a genuine smile or volunteering at a non-profit organization, giving and serving will help you become the best version of yourself as giving and serving will help you grow while making the world a better place. Let me give you an example on how I have served others.

For the past couple of years every Thanksgiving Day I serve the homeless in my community with a local church that I occasionally visit. The impact is so powerful that I have included my best friend and the youth from my nonprofit organization to join me on this day. Some may think that I am crazy because thanksgiving is a day to be at home with family to cook, clean and prepare for the evening traditional dinner –

However – I value serving others before ourselves more. The second year that we served the homeless with our youth all of the kids testified that they no longer cared about what they receive for Christmas or even not caring about their own thanksgiving dinner because they did not realize how many people literally have nothing on this day. We helped prepare a full 3 course meal, packaged it in to-go containers and walked the streets of our community handing the meals out to anyone in need. We not only walked the streets, but we went under every bridge to make sure that no one spent thanksgiving with an empty stomach. In total, we serve about 145 people every year. I recall the smiles, tears and gratitude of the people receiving the packaged foods – a memory I will never forget.

Reflection Time

(Write below or in a journal.)

Take about 20 minutes, technology free and distraction free, to write
what you are most grateful for.

_____
_____
_____
_____
_____
_____
_____
_____
_____
_____
_____
_____
_____
_____
_____
_____
_____
_____
_____
_____
_____
_____
_____
_____
_____
_____

Chapter 2

Living Intentionally

From a very young age, I have always wanted to be the best—the best daughter, the best sister, the best friend, but most importantly, the best at everything I do. Sometimes I think I was born competitive but in a positive way. I have always cared for others and helped them out whenever I could. Growing up in Lawrence, Massachusetts my mother dedicated herself to caring for my brother and I, while my father worked at the Malden Mills, a textile research and development company as a factory worker. My big warm heart filled with love and dedication is a product of the values that were instilled in me by my parents.

At age 7 my parents signed me up to karate, basketball, and softball, and through participating in these sports I quickly learned the value of discipline, hard work, and practice to perfect and perform well. Although my father had never played any of these sports, he always took me to the park to practice on his days off of work. When practicing softball, he would take my fast pitches with his bare hands because he did not know how to use a baseball glove. Now that's dedication! When practicing basketball although he did not know the rules of the game, he helped me practice my offense skills—dribbling, shooting, and moving around the court by simply being present and doing what he knew best, play.

No Excuses

I admired his dedication to my growth; he was intentionally preparing me for success. He never had excuses. Whether he was tired or couldn't communicate to my coaches due to the lack of English, he was always there, and my motivation to succeed came from the desire to make both of my parents proud. My dad used to say that in order to be successful I would have to practice outside of practice. I wanted to be the best, so I practiced outside of practice! I began to dribble my basketball in the house, I would go outside and throw a softball up in the air and catch it when no one was around, I would do this anywhere, even on the way to the grocery store. On weekends I would spend hours with my dad just hitting the softball or shooting some hoops! For Karate, I would stay behind after class and practice with the instructor, this led me to become so advanced that I skipped a karate belt! Shortly after I became a captain and helped my teammates learn routines and practice after class had finished. I loved motivating my friends! I was intentional about growth, and by helping others I was mastering my own skills. I worked hard and received numerous trophies and awards but most importantly the ability to grow with my peers. My mother, my brother Louis, and Dad would cheer me on at games. My family was always there, and by age 9 I felt on top of the world.

In the classroom, I was no different. I knew the value of respect. I respected my teachers, whether they were mean or nice because I was taught by my parents that this is the right thing to do. In school, I respected my peers, I was kind to everyone, I even sat with the kids that sat alone because seeing that made me feel bad. No one should eat alone.

Academically, I was on the honor roll and received several student-of-the-month awards. It felt good to be a great student. My parents always reminded us that getting an education would allow us to be successful in life. I was intent on doing everything possible to do well in the classroom. Even when I would struggle with math (my worst nightmare at the time), I asked for extra tutoring.

Power Comes From Adversity

When I was on the brink of turning 10, my father had a massive stroke that left him paralyzed and non-verbal. One of the biggest parts of my life was shattered. I was with him when the stroke happened, and for the first time in my life I felt helpless and hopeless. To see my father weak and not able to get up killed me inside. Who was going to play basketball with me? Who was going to go to the park with me and help me with my pitching and catch the ball barehanded? Who was going to double dribble around the park's basketball court every weekend? Who was going to give me Daddy advice when I most needed it? Would he still come to my games, even though he was in a wheelchair? Life quickly took a turn on me and I had to learn how to live without him physically being there because we couldn't afford to transport him. Of course, I was too young to understand the cost involved, all I knew was that my dad would never see me play again. I was upset, I was confused, I didn't understand what went wrong. Nothing was the same.

My mother had to work multiple jobs, so I began spending more and more time and the Boys & Girls Club of Lawrence, where I met the associate director and basketball coach, Steve Kelley. Steve is a great man, and I now believe it was destiny for our lives to cross paths. Steve became my lighthouse outside of my home. He ingrained the value of working hard with his famous quote, "Hard work, pays off!" he would tell us. He believed that education was paramount, and, regardless of how good we were athletically, we were benched if we didn't produce good grades in our classes. Our teachers and coaches would send weekly reports that we had to hand into Steve every Friday before games, and we had to study for an hour before practice. Because we all loved basketball, it motivated everyone as a team to do well in school; we were more attentive and aware of our school performance. The basketball team came together as a family and encouraged each other to do well so that we could all play and reach our goal—winning the championship. And that we did! We won the championship!

"I Want To Be Successful!"

By the age of 13, I was hungry for success. I didn't know exactly what I wanted to do, but I knew I wanted to be successful. I wanted to make my mother proud, I wanted to visit my father at the nursing home and tell him about my accomplishments just to see his smile. After one of our practices, I stayed behind to speak Steve. After some small talk, I said, "Steve, I want to be really, really successful, what do I have to do to be successful?" He gave me a big smile and replied, "Joanna, you have so much potential. If you want to be really successful go to college and get your education!" So, I worked even harder to make sure that I was able to go to college. Two weeks into high school there was a gun threat, I ran to the club and, crying, I told Steve that I didn't want to go back. I wanted out, I did not feel safe. Steve suggested that I consider doing a repeat 8th grade year, at first this idea was foreign to me. This is a common action for students that want to apply for private and boarding high schools if they have not done so post 8th grade. So, I went back to 8th grade—not the most popular decision a 13-year-old would be ecstatic about. My so-called friends made hurtful remarks, and I was called "stupid" "retarded" and "whack," but I forgave them because they didn't understand my future the way that Steve Kelley did. Most people would think that success is always moving in a forward direction not backwards, but little did I know that this move backwards, would be more like a slingshot pulling me back for the biggest launch of my life!

One Foot In Front Of The Other

Living intentionally has it perks, it presents opportunities and it brings wisdom and guidance because of the consistency in your life. I kept playing basketball and kept studying, and when it came to applying for high schools, I applied to 10 private and boarding schools, most of which I had never heard of (I never knew you could live at a high school). By coincidence, a school admissions counselor, Gregor McKechnie, from Proctor Academy visited the club on a day I happened to be there, and Steve introduced us. The Boys and Girls Club has great relationships with private schools, and admissions counselors occasionally stop by to say hello. Gregor was a cool, hip guy, he had a little swag and was kind of funny. He told me all about the school and I decided to apply, and within time, I was accepted. I am so grateful to Gregor for taking the time to educate me about the school. My decision to attend Proctor Academy turned out to be one of the best experiences in my life! Hard work really does pays off! By excelling academically, athletically, and within my community by engaging in community service I was able to position myself to land an opportunity of a lifetime. This is when I started to realize the **value of being the best version of myself.** If I did not have good grades or worked hard outside of the classroom, this opportunity would have not opened for me.

I excelled at Proctor, both in the classroom and athletically. I was able to study abroad in Costa Rica, Spain, and France; I never thought in a million years I would be able to experience that. At Proctor Academy, I lived to learn and learned to live throughout the numerous classroom and experiential opportunities. Success was instilled in me by living the school's mission and implementing it in my life by: "Understanding the values of honesty, compassion, respect, and responsibility with strategies to become lifelong learner and thoughtful contributor to my community." (Proctor's Vision Statement)

Reflection Time

Take about 20 minutes, technology free and distraction free, to write how you can become more intentional in your life.

_____

_____

_____

_____

_____

_____

_____

_____

_____

_____

_____

_____

_____

_____

_____

_____

_____

_____

_____

_____

_____

_____

_____

_____

_____

_____

_____

_____

Chapter 3
Be Intentional

What does it mean to be intentional? Moreover, why does it matter? To be intentional means to do things on purpose, to achieve goals, to get a job, to lose weight, apply to college or to accomplish your to-do list. It also means to do things 'Strategically in Order to Land Opportunities' (S.O.L.O), in which strategic actions **move** you into action! You need to be your most prominent advocate and *continuously* seek opportunities, mentorship, and help. One of my biggest advice? Never stop seeking opportunities. The difference between someone who comes across opportunities vs. someone who feels that they never get a chance is: **Intentionality.**

The 4 steps of intentionality are:

1. Identify a need
2. Ask for the opportunity
3. S.O.L.O: Make strategic moves in order to land opportunities
4. Follow-up

Let's break it down:

Step 1. Identify a need. To make progress, you must actively identify areas in your life that need attention.

Examples of Needs: Get a job, seek a tutor or apply to college.

Step 2. Ask for the opportunity. Asking is like shooting basketballs in a hoop, the more you shoot a ball, the more likely you will score, right? Same concept in life – the more you ask for help (or guidance), the higher the chance you will come across an opportunity! Many people give up after a few tries because it may seem too hard, or they may feel that they have no luck. Just remember, opportunities do not come to you, you need to go out and find them, but most importantly, remember it will take time.

Now that you understand, let us implement the 'Ask!'

Let's say you are asking for an opportunity to work in the food industry.

a) Ask your friends if they know of any food restaurants hiring.
b) Post on your social media: "Does anyone know of any restaurants hiring in the area?"
c) Ask teachers and mentors if they know of job openings in this industry. (they may have kids or friends that were recently hired in such places)

Step 3. Make moves Strategically in Order to Land Opportunities (S.O.L.O). This concept is key to your success in landing opportunities. It is essential to be mindful of your actions to create memorable interactions with anyone you engage with. Remember, other people will be looking for similar opportunities, so put your best foot forward and create lasting interactions to increase your chances to land interviews and important meetings. Here are some ideas on strategies you should consider:

*Do this exercise with any goal you have; this example is for looking for a job within restaurants.

a) Write a list of restaurants in your area.
b) Create or polish your resume.
c) Research online to see if there are any openings available and apply. Feel free to call the restaurant to see if they are actively hiring because sometimes the website might not be up to date.
d) Learn about the company's history, mission, values, and services to be ready to engage in a conversation with the manager for your future interview.
e) Visit each of your identified restaurants (dress sharp, make eye contact and smile and have a clean resume copy with you).
f) Meeting the manager? Greet the him/her with positive energy and kindly state that you are currently looking for a job in a restaurant and you wanted to stop by and see if there were any openings available.
g) If there isn't a job opening available, thank them for their time and ask if you can leave your resume for future consideration.
h) If there is an opening, hand them your resume and ask them what is their preferred method of application.
i) Thank them for their time (with a smile) and say you look forward to the opportunity to interview with them soon.
j) Send off job application asap.
This next step is where most people crush their momentum toward opportunities.

The Follow-Up!

Step 4. Follow-up. In any given opportunity, you should attempt to follow-up with the person you were in contact at least 3 times. After speaking to the manager of the restaurant (on your visit), ask them for their email address (or find it online). When you get a chance that day or the day after, send them a thank-you email reiterating your desire to work for them. Finish by saying you look forward to hearing from them. Managers are extremely busy, so do not get discouraged if you do not hear from them right away. Be patient and focus on your other job options.

Follow-up timetable:

- Follow-up 1: Follow-up with the manager via email within the first few days, preferably within 24 hours. This email is your 'Thank you' email; thanking them for their time in speaking with you and letting them know that your application is on its way.
- Follow-up 2: Follow-up with the manager via phone within 7 days from the **last contact** if you have not heard regarding your application as a friendly check in to hear about any updates
- Follow-up 3. Follow up with manager with a phone call within 7 days from **last contact** if you still haven't heard of an update.

Most likely you will have heard by your 2nd to 3rd attempt but keep in mind that looking for a job is like fishing. Keep searching, continue exploring, maintain your energy positive and stay committed – eventually, you will catch your BIG FISH!

Note: Keep all messages short, kind, and positive. Proofread your emails and have someone review them before sending. Good Luck!

Can you commit to yourself?

Can you promise to get up and hunt your opportunity down?

Regardless if you KNOW all the answers or NOT?

Hunt Opportunities Down

Here are a few examples on how I have landed opportunities by simply being intentional; and make a note of the fact that nothing I did required a special skill, or a miracle. All it took was EFFORT. I am ambitious and persistent, and if you are the same, THE WORLD IS YOURS.

Interning at Walt Disney World: I knew I needed to find an internship to graduate my bachelor's program at Lasell College in Newton, Massachusetts. I also knew that I would need to enjoy the internship, so I Googled, "Internships for college students," and BAM! Walt Disney World College Program popped up. I couldn't believe it at first.

An internship?

At Disney?

Paid?

I GET TO WORK WITH MICKEY MOUSE?

I read about the program, the opportunities to engage in college courses, and the benefits I had access to at working at Walt Disney World, a global company! What was my next step?

Action!

There was a deadline for applications, so I sprang into action and filled in all the necessary paperwork. Within a few weeks, I offered a phone interview; it was long, intense but I was prepared! A few weeks passed and I was hired! I interned for the Magic Kingdom and had another experience of a lifetime. Never in a million years could I have ever predicted living in Florida for a year, interning at Disney while taking college courses, getting paid, and having a blast, all at the same time! Again, this is all testament to me striving to be the best version of myself: working hard, excelling academically, getting involved in my community, being intentional and moving into action RIGHT AWAY when opportunities arises. I was prepared to showcase my talents, skills, and experience through a phone call interview all because I was intentional with getting involved at a young age.

My biggest takeaway from working for Disney was that you should always go above and beyond when working with customers or engaging with people. **Regardless** of how you feel; you never know if you are the only person capable of making someone's day; in turn, you will be an excellent employee and become an asset where ever you are employed because of your character and what you bring to the table.

Earning Scholarships: Scholarship organizations, foundations, and individual donors want to make sure that their money is going to be well invested, meaning recipients receiving the support is leveraging the opportunity they receive. What I mean by leveraging the opportunity is positively taking advantage of the opportunity and giving 100% effort in your endeavors that follow. Will the student be engaged in sports? Theatre? Dance? Leadership groups? Volunteer? Do great academically? When I was in middle school and high school, I was actively involved in community projects and services. At the Boys and Girls Club I tutored students, joined a community service club called Keystone, and was active in student government in school; the list goes on. All of this gave me experience, leadership skills, communication skills, and a reputation that would make me stand out as a strong candidate for a scholarship (or any opportunity). Growing up in a low-income family, I knew I would need financial help for college, so I never gave less than 100%.

When the time came to apply for colleges, I approached the college counselor at the club and asked about scholarships for college. She gave me several applications to fill out with specific deadlines and instructions, and I followed through. Hard work pays off! I became a scholarship recipient!

Notice that even before realizing I was intentional, I was intentional. I practiced step by step what I am teaching you about being intentional, which resulted in tremendous success. Till this day I experience accomplishments because of this vital behavior that I practice every day.

Over the years I have applied for many different types of scholarships. Here is how I implemented the 4 steps S.O.L.O strategy mentioned earlier when applying for scholarships.

1. **Identify Need:** Seek Scholarships
2. **Ask for the opportunity:** Find out how to apply and where to find them followed by asking for the person in charge of this resource (in your school, after-school program, coaches or summer camps)
3. **S.O.L.O:** Follow the guidance given, remain in contact with key individuals in charge, apply.
4. **Follow-up:** Follow up with key individuals and maintain this relationship by stopping by their office to say hello and receive any updates.

Was there any luck with this process? No. 100% Intentionality.

The Problem

Opportunities do not fall on your lap; you have to knock on doors, many doors, to find the right opportunities for you and your desired goals. Sometimes it may take weeks, months, or even years to find the right opportunity, but if you don't knock on doors and open them yourself, you will not progress. It is OK to not fully understand how to navigate life or situations, it is NOT OK to procrastinate and refuse to seek guidance from a teacher, mentor, guidance counselor, or even a family member. Another thing to keep in mind is that when you knock on doors and come across opportunities, sometimes these first opportunities are not exactly what you are looking for; however, they can be a stepping stone to get you closer to your ultimate dream job or opportunity by building on experience.

The Sky Is <u>Not</u> The Limit

John Maxwell, a famous American author, speaker, and pastor once said:

"When you live each day with intentionality, there's almost no limit to what you can do. You can transform yourself, your family, your community, and your nation. When enough people do that, they can change the world. When you intentionally use your everyday life to bring about positive change in the lives of others, you begin to live a life that matters."

Read that quote one more time and digest every word.

Let's break this quote down.

"When you live each day with intentionality, there's almost no limit to what you can do."

Of course, there is no limit to what you can do; if you are constantly intentional with what you want. Let's use the restaurant job example from earlier. What should you be doing? You should be polishing or creating a resume, applying for at least 10 jobs a day, check your local newspaper for job listings, checking craigslist's or other job search sites, asking friends if they know of any employers hiring, googling desired jobs in your area, networking and connecting with potential employers (via job fairs), the list goes on. You may think that this is all common sense, but I come across people day in and day out who have this goal in mind and genuinely have no idea on how to proceed forward.

I piloted a goal-setting activity within my organization's Youth Leadership Academy at Top Notch Scholars, Inc., and it blew my mind how, week after week, half of the kids in the group would not do a single thing toward their goals. When asked 'why' they just put their head down and shrugged their shoulders. These kids have great intentions, but still can't seem to understand their full potential nor how to successfully navigate the very tasks needed to complete their goals. By the end of our program 100% of our youth complete their goals identified!

You Have To Want It

There is a girl in my program, let's call her Sheila, who was upset that she couldn't find a job because she was only 15 and most of the places start hiring at 16. Sheila would report to the group week after week frustrated, declaring that she had looked "everywhere." So, I decided to use Sheila's experience and make it into a class exercise. We found out that ice cream shops and supermarkets typically hire 15-year-olds, so as a class we created a list of local places she could contact. One day, by coincidence, we were out on a class trip and happened to find an ice cream shop that was hiring. With a sigh of frustration, Sheila didn't approach the shop because she assumed that they would not hire her. In the end, I took the information from the ice cream shop window and gave it to her. She got the job within days of communicating with the ice cream shop!

I asked her why she hadn't approached ice cream shops and supermarkets during her search, and it turned out that she had given up quite early because she had no hope. All those weeks she was reporting to us that she was not having any success, she wasn't looking! She just **assumed** that if the places she had asked didn't hire 15-year-olds, no one would. The moral of the story? Eliminate assumptions, or they will become the most significant barrier between you and your goals. If a 15-year-old can apply regardless of her negative thoughts, so can you! You will miss all the shots you don't take, if you have an opportunity, take it!

"You can transform yourself, your family, your community, and your nation."

What if you had nothing to lose? Would you go for every opportunity in front of you? Why not? By being intentional, you automatically set yourself up for success because you are continually moving, meeting people, and taking a chance. Being intentional transformed my life, I never thought I would be speaking to thousands of people; inspiring and motivating them toward their peak performance, starting up my own business, creating leadership and job opportunities for kids, writing this book, changing my community for the better, and just becoming a game changer while creating game changers before me. All of this happened because I had a vision and I WANTED IT BAD. I wanted to make a difference, and I did not let anything hold me back. My dreams are more significant than me, and I just told myself to get used to the pressure. The bigger my goals were, the more unique connections I had to make. I grew as an individual, a professional, and an active citizen in my community. I cannot afford to sit down and let days pass me by. The world depends on my vision. I know that if I can impact my community, I can influence the nation. Of course, there are tough days when I feel discouraged or drained, but as long as I get out of my funk and get back on track, this is all that matters! We are all human, after all.

"When enough people do that, they can change the world."

How many people do you think want to change the world? How many people do you think want to change the world and don't know how? How many people do you think want to change the world and don't know how, and therefore give up and end up doing something else that is not aligned with their fire (purpose) that burns within them. Thousands upon thousands of people! We give up on ourselves long before an opportunity is present. Give yourself a chance! When enough people have the courage to make a difference across the nation and globally, change happens. I have heard people say, "I am not good enough," "I am not smart enough," "I have no idea how to start." These are called excuses. You ARE good enough, you ARE smart enough, and if you have no idea how to start:

Get an education and study your passion.

Read relevant books.

Educate yourself.

Research online.

Ask people.

Network.

Pray.

"When you intentionally use your everyday life to bring about positive change in the lives of others, you begin to live a life that matters."

Did you know that everyone on this planet has a purpose? You were put on this earth to fulfill it! I believe that we were not created and placed on this earth by accident. I believe God carefully plans everyone's purpose in life and it is up to us to discover it. A life that matters is a life geared toward making this world a better place, helping those in need and just being a positive force wherever you go. Why not? There is so much power in being intentionally kind, intentionally giving of oneself, intentionally (and genuinely) loving, intentionally compassionate, intentionally conscious of others and their feelings and intentionally thoughtful. The best part of being intentionally amazing? IT'S FREE. It does not cost you a dime to make this world a better place. It is not hard to do either. This concept will automatically make you feel happy and filled with a sense of fulfillment. It isn't an out-of-this-world gesture either. What is your daily routine? What if you aim to make a small gesture a day to make someone smile just by:

- Sharing a compliment
- Holding a door
- Helping someone out with carrying their groceries
- Giving a long-lost friend a call
- Sending a friend, a friendly email
- Buying a friend, a coffee
- Helping someone in need
- Asking a neighbor if they need help with anything
- Letting someone cut you in line at the supermarket because you notice they have fewer items than you
- Helping someone connect with a job you may know about
- The list goes on!

Challenge yourself to be great not just for yourself but for others as well!

Let's be intentional.

- **Triangles:** On the next page identify **8 people** in your life that you want to be intentional toward, such as reaching out and engaging in a small gesture of gratitude. Gestures can include:
  - a phone call to say hello
  - buying flowers or writing a note/email
  - inviting them to the movies or dinner
  - hanging out and catching up

Write the person's name and your gesture in the **triangles around the sun**. Repeat this 2 to 3 times a year, and you will not only feel great and fulfilled, but you are also strengthening your relationships with people near and dear to you.

- **Circle:** In the big circle, on the next page write:
  1. One area in your life that you want to be more intentional in, for example increasing your grades in school, spending time with family, engaging in programs, joining a sport or losing weight.
  2. Describe your 'why.'
     For example, "Spend time with family." It is important to me because they bring me happiness when I am around them. Life is short and spending quality time with them will be my priority moving forward.

Intentionality; A Perfect Example

My best friend, Jenny Alvarez, is a prime example of going above and beyond and being intentional in helping others. Jenny is always thinking of others and how she can connect someone to something to help overcome their struggle. We have a running joke that when she is talking to someone, as soon as she identifies a need or struggle, she is like an online search engine; her mind goes a million miles per second resulting in a billion solutions or resources. We might as well create a search engine in her name. There is value when you allow yourself to be conscious of those around you, after all, if you were ever struggling, wouldn't you want people to be thinking of ways to help you?

A Lifestyle With A Purpose

Jenny is the CEO of J. Alvarez and Company, an event planning and production company geared toward event planning, decor, coordinating, budget planning, and most recently offering event gowns for sweet 15s, proms, weddings, and special occasions. Jenny focuses on really getting to know her clients and their needs, so that she can provide a memorable event. Jenny says that her event-planning business is just a tool to connect to people and help them out in any way possible. Many times, she comes across parents that need help with their teenager regarding socioemotional issues, motivation, or overall life path, she quickly educates them about us at Top Notch Scholars, so that we can work on developmental skills while connecting them with any other community resources that best fit their needs.

One day, Jenny had a client who was planning a sweet 16 for her daughter who had recently lost her father to cancer. The mother had lost her job shortly after the death in the family and she was struggling. She couldn't afford the party her daughter deserved, and she was sad that her little girl would never get to dance with her dad for the traditional father-daughter dance. To make up for the loss of her father's presence, Jenny came up with the mother-daughter dance idea, which was a huge success. Jenny also tapped into her professional network to connect the mother with a job. The mother was able to plan the party of her daughter's dream event Afterall, and the daughter was ecstatic about the memory she was able to create with her loved ones.

Create Your Happiness

Sometimes we are in a situation that makes us feel useless or disconnected. It is very essential to get in the habit to seek your happiness even if we don't feel great. Let's continue with 'having a job' as an example. If you have a job that rarely interacts with people (and working with people fulfills you) – be very intentional with your time outside of work. You can easily connect with nonprofit organizations and causes outside of work. Make time in your schedule to volunteer at an organization or a church, tutor a child, take part in city organized cleaning efforts, volunteer to play board games with the elderly at a nursing home, serve dinner at a food pantry, and so on. What drives you? Whether it's our job or an extracurricular activity that we engage in, there is always time to give a helping hand, and when we give, we become connected with a greater cause that is beyond ourselves.

Happiness is not necessarily living every day as if it were a party nor is it being surrounded with friends every second of the day. Happiness DEFINITLEY is not about how many likes or followers you have on social media. Happiness is having a healthy balance of what truly makes you happy. Do you know what makes you happy? One way I create my happiness is – I may decide to go on a bike ride as I know nature soothes my soul. I may ask my friends if they want to join me to ride a trail & if they are not available, I am quick adjust my plans by riding my bike in the city instead because it is be a safer option for me. Regardless, I will **still go** and do what makes me happy. Just because my ideal plan didn't work out doesn't mean I turn to do nothing or turn to do something that would hurt me. If I ever feel bummed out, I think of things that may cheer me up and I go do that. The point? We should never sit here and drown in our misery; if we don't create our own happiness who will? Avoid getting together with friends and fueling the fire by complaining as this will only make you feel worse.

Another important note: Happiness is not found in OTHERS (boyfriends, girlfriends, friends), it is found within OURSELVES. Be in alignment with what makes you feel amazing and keep doing that! In the moments that you are down, the storm doesn't last forever, and there will be a new day. We ALL have bad days, failures, experience rude/not so nice people, do poorly on a test or feel sluggish at times but this does not dictate our future - it's just a part of life – Enjoy the rollercoaster!

Reflection Time

- Take about 20 minutes, technology free and distraction free, to write about possible things you would like to do to give back to your community or a cause. (Example: Become a volunteer at your local pet shelter, kids' club, or become a mentor.)
- Once you have identified what you would like to do, write about why this is important for you and how it will make you feel.

_____
_____
_____
_____
_____
_____
_____
_____
_____
_____
_____
_____
_____
_____
_____
_____
_____
_____
_____
_____
_____
_____
_____
_____

"The future depends on what we do in the present." — Mahatma Gandhi

Chapter 4

Believe in Yourself

$\mathcal{T}$his chapter is my favorite concept because I already know what the result is when someone sincerely believes in themselves. I am a product of believing. Once you realize that YOU ARE IN CONTROL of your life, it will take a turn toward its fullest potential. Throughout this chapter, I have handpicked a few quotes regarding self-belief that I have enjoyed. Gandhi clarified the power we have within ourselves when he stated: "Change yourself, you are in control."

After working with several students and professionals, studying the psychology of human performance through my Ph.D. Program, and, of course, personal experience, I have concluded that there is a common reason why people can't seem to reach their goals, and that is the lack of self-belief, also known as having low self-esteem. Way before a person comes close to achieving a grain of success; they close the door on themselves because of the negative thoughts, doubts and self-destructive beliefs. Most of the time, these thoughts are self-cultivated and once it's in their subconscious mind it is downhill from there. Why do we doubt ourselves? Why do people turn to this destructive mental practice? Who said that negative thoughts equal truth? The mind is so powerful! Studies have shown that just by the thought of something, it can start the process of bringing it to life. If you think you are not good enough, you will not feel good enough, therefore in your mind, you truly are not good enough. It's crazy how the mind and body play a role in your belief system.

Buddha once said, "What you think, you become. What you feel, you attract. What you imagine, you create." What have been your most common thoughts about yourself? Are they negative or positive? Whatever those thoughts are, I guarantee you feel and attract just that. The reason why it is important to recognize how you perceive yourself is because the images in your head about yourself create a glass ceiling; an invisible cap on your potential, and only you have the power to remove it. Due to the fact you may think and feel a certain way about yourself, achieving goals in certain areas of your life may FEEL impossible because of the way you SEE yourself. You may say to yourself, "I can never do that, I am not qualified enough," "I can never work for that company, I am not good enough," or my favorite one, "I do not want to go to college, I am not smart enough, it's too much." WHO SAID YOU ARE NOT GOOD ENOUGH? If a family member or friend told you these negative remarks, that is their opinion; it is not a FACT. Negative remarks stem from envy, jealousy, or internal battles they may be personally struggling with. Why do bullies like to hurt other people? It makes them feel good to make others feel inferior and see others suffer; it all comes down to inner battles. Chapter 7 talks about your bubble, and the importance of whom you surround yourself with. This concept plays a huge role in self-esteem. My favorite comedian has a comedy segment about self-confidence, and it is as true as it gets. He talks about "how you should stop waiting for people to validate who you are." Self-esteem is the esteem of oneself; therefore, how you feel should solely stem from how YOU evaluate yourself, not from the input of others. He goes on to discuss how people tend to blame others because of the way that they feel or the events that have happened to them. Again, they reiterate that self-esteem has nothing to do with other people and to stop worrying about things that do not matter. Stop blaming your partner, your family, the government, the economy, your friends. There are millions of solutions to every problem, but when you focus on things that you cannot control you will end up drowning in a cup of water.

Be grateful for your life, it is short and beautiful, and the possibilities and memories are endless; however, only YOU are in control of how you react to the negative events around you and how you choose to navigate life. Pick yourself up and start loving yourself because it all starts with you! On the flipside, if you are a procrastinator and cannot accomplish things because of a lack of follow-through and lack of communication skills, this is not a reflection on your potential as a person, you just need to improve on certain aspects of your life to get different results. I say this because I often come across people who can't seem to get a job, finish school, or accomplish minor things in life, and when you observe their daily habits and behaviors, they are doing absolutely nothing toward their tasks. Most of the time their priorities are out of whack, and they do not have enough focus and discipline to get things done.

Understand Your Power

According to research, the probability of you being born and existing was 1 in 400 trillion! There is no other human being like YOU. You are here, and you have a future ahead of you. Your life could be gone in an instant, so why not leave doubts, fears, and worries to the side while you attempt this thing called life with happiness? What is the worst thing that can happen? You might fall? Learn from your mistakes and find another way to achieve whatever you want to achieve.

YOU ARE VALUABLE, and this world is lucky to experience your presence. The moment you understand your value and power, you will have the motivation and find the effort to put toward what you desire. If you don't realize your potential, you will never have the energy or effort to work on you. Sometimes people get in the way of your self-esteem and I get it, it can really hurt and throw us off track. Eleanor Roosevelt once said, "No one can make you feel inferior without your consent." If you understand that statement, you will realize that no matter how hurtful people may be to you during your life, only YOU can allow it to break you. Never believe what people say about you because their opinion doesn't matter or pay will ever your bills.

Now that we understand that people's opinions are not facts, how do you talk to yourself?

Watch What You Say

A good chunk of our mind is consumed with ever-changing emotions, impulsive thoughts, and bad habits that lead to procrastination. At times, it can be a lot to deal with, but the most important person we need to take care of is ourselves. We spend 100% of our time with ourselves, so we need to be conscious of not just how we talk to others but also how we speak to ourselves. As cheesy as this sounds, it can make you or break you! We are always judging and making decisions according to our perceived thoughts. What are the conversations that go on in your head? Do you motivate yourself to keep pushing? Alternatively, do you put yourself down? When you are positive, you build yourself up, leading you to perform better and feel better. If you are trash talking yourself you are making yourself feel worthless every day, pointing you towards depression, a sense of loss hope, and (the feeling of) lack of life fulfillment. This can be dangerous.

To make drastic changes, we must shift the way you talk and think about yourself. It's a must. Whether you are a rich celebrity or an average joe, negative self-talk destroys people. The way we think about ourselves is closely related with the way we talk to ourselves. By changing the way we talk to ourselves we can shift the way we think about ourselves. We all have daily stressors, either personal life, work, school, or social stress, why be the creator of more anxiety and sadness? Don't be self-destructive; there is no need for that negativity.

Baby Steps Toward Believing in Yourself

1. **Be Your Biggest Champion:** You may be asking yourself, how can I change? How can I start loving myself? The answer is simple. Be your cheerleader, your motivator, your own HYPE MAN! If you don't love yourself and cheer yourself on, who will? Get in the habit of smiling and patting yourself on the back when you accomplish things, even if it is small, like losing 3 pounds or acing a class. Never let your successes, even minor ones, go unnoticed. Let's go!!!!

2. **Stop Comparing Yourself:** Society is overflowing with reality TV constantly looking at the lives of others and indirectly putting us down because we can't seem to measure up. Comparing your life to others' is pointless because everyone goes through their battles and then chooses what to showcase on social media whether it's true or not. The only person you should be paying attention to is YOU. You will never improve by comparing yourself to others; in fact, you get better by focusing on getting **you** to the next level. Remember, life is not a race; it's a journey toward being the best version of you.

3. **Building Others, Builds You:** Serving others is huge for me. I have built compost holes and gardens for an orphanage in Ecuador, tutored kids, helped in churches, and much more. For me, nothing is more gratifying than helping others and humbling myself by recognizing that others at times are in a worse situation than me and that I can

build them up. By supporting and building others, you are not only making a difference to them, but you are also building yourself up. There is something special about just pouring greatness into the lives of others. You gain experience, solve issues, and become a resource to someone in need. Making others feel good gives off a reciprocal effect of making you feel good. Building others builds character, a connection, and a sense of belonging because you belong here. The world needs you.

4. **Break Your Glass Ceiling:** Repeat after me: "I am my biggest barrier in life." Let this be one of the biggest takeaways from this book. One of the primary reasons why people do not accomplish goals and progress in life is because they give up. Remember that glass ceiling I talked about earlier? Well, imagine looking up and seeing ALL your possibilities and dreams, your potential and the change of lifestyle because of your successes. We don't want to just look, we want to break the ceiling through right now! So, believe and act.

5. **Be You:** I hear young people say that they do nonsense things just to fit in. I have listened to adults admit that they spend too much money going out multiple times a week just to fit in with co-workers. This happens on all levels. The best thing that you can do to build up your self-esteem and progress in the journey of believing in yourself is BEING YOURSELF. When you finally make choices according to your value system you will feel genuine, strong, and solid. If you identify your core values within your relationships, friendships, and family - your personal choices; short- and long-term decisions will begin to start feeling of value. If you don't, you will end up like that inflatable dancing guy/gal outside of car dealerships (out of control).

Don't be an inflatable dancing guy/gal.

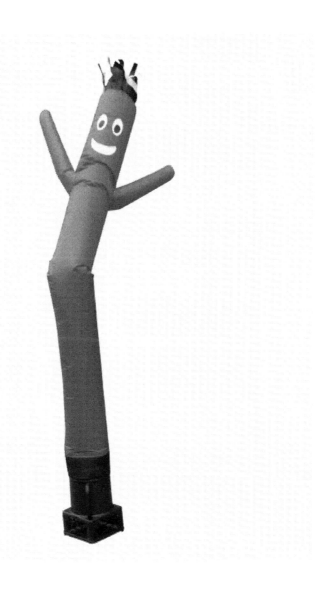

6. **Stop Doubting Yourself:** Self-belief and self-doubt truly control you. I once tutored a 6-year-old named Mandy. One day, Mandy asked me to help her with her homework. Mandy was insecure when it came to doing schoolwork and preferred to have someone help her. On this particular day, she was doing math homework; basic adding and subtracting. I assured Mandy that she was brilliant and that she did not need my help. After fussing, and whining for my assistance, I helped her. All I did was relay the math problem to her verbally and kindly asked her what the answer was. With no hesitation at all, she started to answer the math problem back to back. Mandy did not need my help, yet she was giving up on her task before even trying. Moral of the story? Sometimes we look at life tasks, challenges, and scenarios and automatically tell ourselves we cannot do them before we even try. Mandy is a perfect example of how many of us are wired. We need to stop doubting ourselves the moment we feel insecure or feel challenged. I encourage you to:

- Step 1: Genuinely TRY.
- Step 2: Once you try, the next step is to ASK for assistance. Whom can you ask? A friend, a neighbor, a teacher, a partner, a parent, a family member, a coach, or a co-worker - Anyone willing to help, listen, or guide you.
- Step 3: Repeat until the task is complete.

7. **Own It:** Own your mistakes, own your bad habits, and own your bad choices by recognizing that you are entirely in control. Situations may get tough, unbearable, and maybe feel impossible,

but when you OWN IT, you leave no other option but to tackle it head on and conquer your fears. Whatever you are going through, I want to let you know that you are capable, and as soon as you build the courage to stand up… you will rise. Your life will catapult you toward success, and you will find your purpose. Regardless of your past, it is history, it does not define you or your future. I don't care if you have a bad reputation, have regularly made mistakes, or just never believed in yourself. Starting today, you can begin having control and make the necessary changes to OWN IT.

To Wrap Up Check Out What Other Authors, Entrepreneurs and Even the Bible Say About The Importance Of Believing:

"Twenty years from now, you will be more disappointed by the things you didn't do than by the ones you did do. So, throw off the bowlines. Sail away from the safe harbor. Catch the trade winds in your sail. Explore. Dream. Discover."
– Mark Twain

"You don't become what you want, you become what you believe."
— Oprah Winfrey

"Whatever the mind of man can conceive and believe, it can achieve."
– Napoleon Hill

"Nothing is impossible, the word itself says 'I'm possible!'"
– Audrey Hepburn

Bible Verses
"For God gave us a spirit not of fear but of power and love and self-control."
– Timothy 1:7

"If you believe, you will receive whatever you ask for in prayer."
– Matthew 21:22

Reflection Time

Take about 20 minutes, technology free and distraction free, to write about how you will OWN IT. Write about what changes you will do to start believing in yourself more (self-talk, self-love, etc.)

_____

_____

_____

_____

_____

_____

_____

_____

_____

_____

_____

_____

_____

_____

_____

_____

_____

_____

_____

_____

_____

_____

_____

_____

_____

_____

Chapter 5

Develop Self-Awareness 24/7

To develop and continuously grow, both personally and professionally, knowing who you are is critical. What makes you happy, angry, sad, excited? What are you good at? What are you not good at? Who makes you feel good? Who doesn't make you feel good? Self-awareness is like the dashboard of a vehicle that tells you, the driver, the status of the car. Does the car need gas? Maintenance? Is it overheating? What can you say about yourself by observing? Knowing yourself makes life easier to navigate because you will always have a clear understanding of your emotions, values, passions, and a projected vision of your future. Once you know your vehicle (your body) well enough then you will know how to proceed day to day.

The Importance Of Being Aware

There is a real value in being aware. As you go through your day, week, month, and year, you will want to know where you are right now to plan for the future. I start these conversations as early as sixth grade. It is impossible to prepare for the future if you are unsure about your life, interests, and desires. If you are not entirely in tune with yourself, you wind up winging life and taking things as they come. What if you could cut your social media consumption down and do things that nurture your soul like reflecting and exploring? Society is so distracted by social media, the news, external drama that do not involve us, binging on Netflix shows for hours, wasting our time on relationships that are clearly not good for us, buying material things that have no value, or smoking and drinking that leads us to burn our precious valuable time away. It is impossible to waste your life away *and* expect your life to be on point, ready for success with opportunities at your door.

Think, Develop, Grow!

One of the most effective ways to develop self-awareness is through a system I created; the **Think, Develop, Grow** process.

THINK: Get ready for success to start pouring into your life. However, first, let's prepare and get ready for the process. When consulting students or my professional clients, I always recommend being intentional about setting some time aside from work, school, and social life for themselves - The same way we make time for Netflix, Keeping up with the Kardashians, sports, and any other extra-curricular activities. I suggest thinking of spaces that relax you where you can think freely at peace, **alone**. The reason why I emphasize alone is that if you are with people; A.) there is a mixture of energy, B.) a pressure of leaving by a particular time, and C.) possible distractions. This time is for you and only you. During my moments of reflection, I like to go on bike rides, kayak, go to the gym with headphones, go on a car ride, hike, or stay home. When you are alone, put your phone on silent and intentionally ignore it unless it is an emergency. **Disclaimer:** Don't worry; your social media will still be there when you are done. When all distractions are out of sight, take the time to think. While thinking, use a notebook and write down where you are and where you want to go. It doesn't have to be perfect; it can be ideas. The purpose of this exercise is to get your mind, career and destiny in sync with what you desire. Once you identify these areas, you will become more apparent on where you need to go, what resources you need and what changes you need to make. Feel free to write down habits that will block you from achieving your goals and identify why is it important for you to make these changes. Now that you have come up with where you would like to go, it's time for step two. Keep in mind that this is not a one-day process. This exercise takes anywhere from a few weeks to a year if you are consistent with always thinking about your desired future. Your desired future does not need to be a career goal; it can be education, fitness goal, health goals or mastering a skill that you've always wanted to further.

DEVELOP: Your possible path has been well thought out, now it's time to set the foundations needed to take off. Let's use a career goal, for example. You have identified that you would like to be in the healthcare field, but you are not quite sure exactly where. While brainstorming you had a vision of you working in the emergency room, maybe being a surgeon, yet you didn't quite like the idea of blood and the pressure of being responsible for someone's life. You have also identified that you are more of a behind-the-scenes kind of person. You've also determined that you enjoy the more technical side of things within healthcare; maybe in IT or working with patients' results.

Another thing you have identified is your ideal salary. You have brainstormed that living in New England can get quite expensive; you want to buy a house and live comfortably. Through your research online you came up with an average salary of $60k to $70k to be very conservative but realistic to support a family. Now it's time for the next step.

GROWTH: You now have a foundation, an idea, now it's time to dig further! At this point, I would recommend you start having conversations with people and institutions. Visit a college and ask to speak to a guidance counselor and express your initial thoughts on what you think you want to do. (You can do this at any age, it does not cost money to speak to someone). They will be able to help identify possible career tracks that best suit your desires and passions. Since you did your due diligence in digging within yourself and what you are most interested in; the easy part is learning what's available. The counselor discusses several options, and being a radiologist peaks your interest. As you ask more questions and find out that entry-level radiology technicians make about $40,000+, and by continuing your education you can become a general radiologist, where the salary is over $200,000. Now, we are starting to see a clear path of success and can visually see the path of growth! With the connections of the college, their network, and maybe your network (mentors), you can now be intentional about scheduling a visit to meet a radiologist or get permission to visit a room where the work takes place just to experience it firsthand. Once you have made your decision on pursuing this career, what's next? GROW!

Reflection Time

Are there any areas right now in your life that you need some time to reflect and research in order to have a clearer vision of your life path?

_____

_____

_____

_____

_____

_____

_____

_____

_____

_____

_____

_____

_____

_____

_____

Are there any workshops, training, or education that you need to further your goals identified?

This may include college, trade school, certificates, etc.

_____
_____
_____
_____
_____
_____
_____
_____
_____
_____
_____
_____
_____
_____
_____

Once you have completed the training, workshops, or education needed

Name your upcoming successes below.

Examples - I will be a master chef, I will open my own business, I will be able to become a personal trainer. Be very detailed when discussing your success. Also include location of your ideal employment or business, your title and accomplishment.

_____
_____
_____
_____
_____
_____
_____
_____
_____
_____
_____
_____
_____
_____

Chapter 6

The Power of Proactiveness

*I*f you want a sense of control over your life, your emotions, and how scenarios play out, being proactive is key. Proactiveness isn't a behavior that you are naturally born with; it is a skill that you learn and master until it becomes a way of being. Let's break down some of the qualities of a proactive person. A proactive person…

- Typically lives life without excuses
- Gets things done without anyone asking
- Takes responsibility for their life
- Usually, are ambitiously 5 steps ahead of their own decisions
- Does not react impulsively in situations
- Is calm, collected, level headed and conscious of others
- Strategically thinks decisions through
- "Owns it."

The benefits of being a proactive person is that you are in control because you are always thinking ahead. A person that thinks ahead can plan ahead, and therefore is always prepared for what's to come or worst-case scenarios.

Always Have A Game Plan

If you had to drive cross country from Massachusetts to California, would you drive without a roadmap or GPS? Most likely not. It is crucial for you to know what your roadmap of life looks like, and that starts by thinking and planning. I like to mentor the mindset of having a plan on top of a plan. Why should you over plan? Because if plan A didn't quite work out the way you envisioned it, you have a plan B. Worst-case scenario, if plan B doesn't work out, well at least you've thought of a plan C. If you do not think of alternative strategies, who will?

I am passionate about teaching people, especially youth, the power of being proactive because this is an intentional behavior to ensure that you reach the highest chances of success regardless of your background, economic status and your current situation; whether it is landing a job, passing a test or preparing for something important. Check out how I prepare today's youth on how to be proactive with their life to position themselves for their ultimate success personally and professionally.

I met Tommy when he was a 15-year-old sophomore in high school; we started talking about his interests, likes, dislikes, and possible future career. We discussed the importance of being proactive, planning, and gaining experience early, and how it would benefit him in the long run by having a strong resume at an early age, and the buildup of work ethic & character. Tommy liked the idea!

Tommy and I identified that he had an interest in being a veterinarian because he loves and cares for animals dearly. With my resources and connections, I set up an appointment for Tommy at a local veterinarian hospital to shadow a Vet for a day. He loved the hands-on experience! This opportunity was a confirmation for Tommy that this field was the right one for him in the future. Due to Tommy's age, however, he could not work or intern there, but he could volunteer. Tommy started to volunteer once a week until he turned 16 and a half in which the opportunity for him to intern opened up at the hospital as he nurtured the relationship overtime! He was ecstatic with joy! Tommy continued to intern there up until his senior year of high school, and by the age of 18 he had 3 years of experience volunteering and interning at a veterinarian hospital, while he discovered his passion and purpose in life!

Tommy went on to college with a clear vision on what he wanted to study. Tommy's peers did not tap into their passions, interests, or build any sort of experience. At the end of high school, many of Tommy's peers were undecided in what to study, some chose not to go to college, and some started with a major and quickly discovered that the areas of study they chose were not what they wanted to do. For his peers in this process, financial aid funds were wasted, and additional loan was accumulated due to switching majors and ending up on a longer track to graduate. The model I used with Tommy is the same model I use to position youth to build their resume and experience, and it has been a huge success. This is the "S.O.L.O" Theory as mentioned earlier in the book (Making moves **S**trategically in **O**rder to **L**and **O**pportunities)!

Tommy has a bright future. Be like Tommy.

Do Not Go With The Flow

If we are proactive with our future, we have the chance to iron things out by exploring ourselves and come across opportunities that we otherwise wouldn't come across. There is nothing wrong with allocating social and fun time for oneself; however, it is not OK to let life pass you by because you are living in the moment and not thinking of your future.

Only **<u>Dead</u>**

FISH

Go with the

FLOW

-Andy Hunt

Don't be a dead fish.

Proactive Versus Reactive

The opposite of proactive is reactive. The significant difference between the two is that by being proactive, as you know, you are in control of your situation by planning, responding with ease, and thinking ahead. However, by being reactive, situations **control** you, leading you to react to things without thinking. There are two circumstances where you can be proactive and reactive, and they are:

- In your personal life
- Outside your personal life

Being proactive in your personal life means that:

- You plan ahead, and you are always moving forward
- You prioritize important tasks
- You take care of yourself and your mental stability
- You are all about business – you execute!

Being proactive outside your personal life means that:

- You are always thinking of others and make yourself available to help
- Participate with others in special activities or events
- Help others even if they do not ask
- Remain in control even when things get out of control

Being reactive in your personal life means that:

- You blame others for your failures

- Your blame your environment for the lack of your success
- Other people's negative reactions will ruin your day
- You often focus on issues rather than solutions.

Being reactive outside your personal life means that:

- You react according to the flow of life
- You react before analyzing a situation thoroughly
- Everything in your surroundings affects you

I highly recommend that if you identify with being a reactive person, start taking baby steps to think before you speak, even in the toughest scenarios. It comes down to having a positive outlook on life 24/7, seeing the bigger picture and, of course, being the bigger person. A reactive person leads a stressful and chaotic life, and they always seem to blame others, their environment and go with the flow in life.

Let's explore how being a reactive person can truly cause further issues that you may not expect:

On a bright sunny Sunday, you take a drive in your town to catch a breeze and pick up something to eat. Nothing is more perfect than the wind blowing through your hair, the smell of the summer breeze, your favorite tunes are playing, and the sky is blue. You are 5 minutes away from your destination and you stop at a traffic junction. Out of nowhere, BAM! You get hit from behind by another car. Your head hits the airbag, your neck is starting to hurt, and you get out of the car to see what is going on. A sassy lady comes out of the other vehicle and starts yelling at you and accusing you of stopping suddenly. A proactive person would diffuse the situation by speaking to the woman with kindness and pointing out the stop sign ahead. The proactive person would calmly seek solutions by dialing the police and a tow truck. Being cool, calm, and collected allows the individual at fault to calm down and cooperate. However, a reactive person would have got out of the vehicle and added fuel to the fire by lashing back, saying inappropriate words or getting physical. This would only lead to a bigger altercation that would not result in any possible solutions.

The moral of the example is in any given situation think before you speak and even if you are not in the wrong, be kind and humble.

Remember…

"Life is 10% what happens to you and 90% of how you react to it." – Charles Swindoll

Reflection Time

Take about 20 minutes, technology free and distraction free to write how you can become more proactive with your day-to-day living.

_____

_____

_____

_____

_____

_____

_____

_____

_____

_____

_____

_____

_____

_____

_____

_____

_____

_____

_____

_____

_____

_____

_____

_____

Chapter 7

Your Bubble

our bubble is sacred. Your bubble shall be protected. Your bubble is another term for the people that surround you. Family and friends typically exist in your bubble, or what I like to call your CIRCLE OF INFLUENCE. It is super important to know whom you associate yourself with and whom you spend your time with because I guarantee you that your circle will make or break you. Growing up in an inner city, I have seen it all, hung out with all types of people, and was blessed to observe and recognize the importance of who you genuinely keep around you. Let's face it; people will hurt you, talk bad about you, disappear when you most need them, change their air when they are around other types of people, manipulate situations, look for you only when they need you, and even take from you all while smiling in your face. This behavior may include family. It is so important to protect yourself from people who do not value you because YOU ARE VALUABLE.

Have you experienced people that you do not feel at ease around? Have you ever confronted people that may have disrespected you? Do you keep these negative people around you? Be very aware, it will benefit you to constantly observe those around you because by doing this you are protecting your career, mind, and destiny.

Red Flags

In all personal relationships and friendships, there are red flags that we should pay attention to. Red flags are signs that clearly show disrespect, manipulation, or habits of unhealthy treatment. Most of the time people notice it and brush it off, or in some cases, the person may not know that there are healthy options to end a toxic relationship. In 2013, I conducted a short survey with an eighth-grade class to identify if they stay in friendships that are toxic and why. Many admitted that they did not want to hurt the person's feelings, others said that they did not know how to walk away, and the rest of the class stated that they did not know why they haven't removed the toxic friend.

I encourage you to build up the courage to stand up for what you deserve. From kids to adults, we all battle with people who do not treat us the greatest, and let me tell you, you are not obligated to stay in circles that put you down or do not support you. I am not saying get up and leave completely, but control how involved those select individuals are in your life, there is nothing wrong with casual conversations here and there, but your bubble is nothing to play with! If they are extremely toxic to your life, stay woke/be aware.

Life does not come with a manual, but we can do a very good job by selecting those who can be an asset to our life and vice versa. The most valuable move I made throughout my life was to pay attention to those close and far, and how they made me feel. People can tell you all the great things verbally, but what they do in silence speaks louder than words. Someone can tell you that they love you and care for you until they turn around and speak poorly of you or bring nothing but drama to your life. Never has it been written in the bible or any book on life that we must keep toxic people in our immediate life; therefore, make the necessary changes. It can save your life!

There is this girl named Janet who was in a relationship that was abusive and controlling. When I asked her why she stayed in the relationship she looked away and said, "He loves me." The guy would hit her, verbally abuse her, control her cellphone and social media, control whom she went out with, and would get jealous when people would text her, especially other guys. She went on to say that after any physical arguments he would cry, apologize, and say he will make things better. She noted that physical abuse had become worse over the years, but she just didn't know what to do. He went to the extent of taking her online passwords and monitoring her every move while expressing that he would kill himself if she ever broke up with him. I talked to her about how her situation was not healthy and pointed out how it was affecting her school and other personal relationships. After speaking to her about how unhealthy her situation was, I learned that the reason why she tolerated the abuse was due to her insecurity and lack of confidence. She did not value herself. I know this because in previous conversations she shared that she was not pretty, not smart, and could never get a better boyfriend. She was afraid of being alone. She felt important in this relationship despite the abuse and control. Year after year, she kept herself in this unhealthy relationship. She recognized that she needed a change in her life. We created a plan that involved a counselor and her parents to build up her self-confidence and get on a healthier path. We discussed her values, her strengths, what she deserves, her priorities that consisted of school and work and all of the amazing things that are coming her way if she continues to work hard with a healthy state of mind. Within a few months, she was free from the relationship and she was glowing. I was happy for her and her new start.

This message is geared toward those of you reading this book that does not feel good enough. Do not feel that you have to stay in relationships or friendships just because outside of the really bad times they cause - they are nice, or they make you feel good. People will manipulate situations and quickly try to make it better. Someone that respects and loves you will RESPECT AND LOVE YOU 100% of the time, not when they feel like it. I have zero tolerance toward people who try to make me feel bad, offend me, steal from me, control me, hate me, speak poorly of me, make me feel worthless, etc. If people cannot respect you, they do not deserve ANY of you. Not your time, not your presence. You deserve greatness, seek those that want to treat you with dignity.

Let 'Em Go

Tyler Perry, a famous American actor, playwriter, and filmmaker has a comedy series featuring Madea, a tough elderly black female character full of wisdom. While in college I came across one of Madea's video clips that highlighted the value of friendship and when is it time to let people go. This clip helped shift my mindset on how I categorized people in my life and strengthened my views on my belief system regarding human behavior. I have been a victim in believing that every single person in my circle is my best friend or a good friend and that they would never hurt me. Time after time, I gave myself 100% to everyone I called my friend. As you develop and experience the different types of people that filter through your life you quickly notice that not everyone has the right intention, some may become temporary people in your life, and a very small handful become your core circle. I always give people the benefit of the doubt to showcase what a good friend they are, but it is important to stay attentive and protect yourself from unfortunate events and people.

The following used to be my outlook on friendships:

- Everyone will always have my back, why wouldn't they?
- My "friends" would never do anything to backstab, manipulate or use me
- Friendships are forever
- Relationships are forever

I quickly realized this was not true!

Madea breaks people down into three categories: leaf people, branch people, and root people. I learned about the different types of people using her analogy of a tree:

Leaf People

Some people come into your life and they are like leaves on a tree. They are only there for a season. You can't depend on them or count on them because they are weak and only there to give you shade. Like leaves, they are there to take what they need and as soon as it gets cold or wind blows in your life they are gone. You can't be angry at them, it's just who they are.

Branch People

There are some people who come into your life and they are like branches on a tree. They are stronger than leaves, but you have to be careful with them. They will stick around through most seasons, but if you go through a storm or two in your life it's possible that you could lose them. Most times they break away when it's tough. Although they are stronger than leaves, you have to test them out before you run out there and put all your weight on them. In most cases, they can't handle too much weight. But again, you can't be mad with them, it's just who they are.

Root People

If you can find some people in your life who are like the roots of a tree, then you have found something special. Like the roots of a tree, they are hard to find because they are not trying to be seen. Their only job is to hold you up and help you live a strong and healthy life. If you thrive, they are happy. They stay low key and don't let the world know that they are there. Their job is to hold you up come what may, even an awful storm, and to nourish you, feed you, and water you. – Madea, Tyler Perry

Surround Yourself With Lions

People that are positive, uplifting, loving, caring, compassionate, loyal, motivating, and supportive are lions. My circle of lion's hustle, work hard, are focused, and carry zero ounces of drama; when we get together it is nothing but powerful conversations about life, career, and goals. Our friendships consist of brainstorming on how we can help one another other, share resources, and being present during tough times providing a positive support system. Nothing more, nothing less.

Disclaimer: You will not find many people like this in your immediate circle; if you are lucky you may find 2 or 3 people. The rest of your circle will be identified as acquaintances.

I noticed that when I was around people that complained, they did not have any life goals, or simply took life day by day without progression, I was drained. I felt like a puzzle piece attempting to be put in place backward, I didn't fit. I didn't fit because I had different values and outlooks on life. I did not talk about others, I did not complain about life, or engage in activities that wasted time or may affect my health. I knew my value system very well!

While growing up and in college I happened to be in the presence of people smoking cigarettes or other substances; however, I always made it clear that I did not do those things. I was respected, and they never asked again. The moment I was slightly pressured, I would leave. Making your values clear from the beginning in any given relationship is very important because it makes it easier to set the expectation and observe who is not respecting your decisions. Often times, people end up in situations and get pressured by their so-called friends; whether it's just one time or not, **it's not cool**. Let me make this clear. If your "friend" pressures you into doing things that do not align with your values, they are not a true friend. These are signs that allow you the opportunity to make your decisions to move on and recognize whom you are surrounded by.

Lions hang out in packs for a reason because they are stronger together, and together they achieve greatness. I know you are seeking and chasing to be great, so hang with great. Anything less than this will drag you down, demotivate you, and set you back 10 steps. Protect your bubble and hang with your lions.

Ten ways to identify lions around you:

★ Lions want to see you succeed
★ Lions are focused on their success and they will always be willing to help you achieve your goals
★ Lions focus on solutions when they encounter obstacles
★ Lions are loyal, trustworthy, and genuine
★ Under pressure and disappointment, a lion will never give up on you
★ Lions will stand up for you
★ Lions never settle for less and continue to fight for what they want
★ Lions will always find a way to be there for you, without excuses
★ Lions will always look out for your best interest
★ Lions become family

How To Filter Out Those Bad Influences

I often get asked, "How do you remove people in your life that are bad influences?" I love this question because it is easier than you think! Now, there is no need to tell them to their face that you are cutting them off. Off the bat, you know what your values are and what you like and don't like, right? Watch how I would turn down activity from someone who most likely will invite me to do the same thing over and over and I do not want to engage in their activities. The underlined sections below can be substituted with any action.

Example

Friend: "Hey come over, let's hang out and smoke hookah!"

You: "Hey, I can't, I'm actually working on an idea to create my own business. Why don't you come over? I have so many ideas that could totally take off and go viral!"

Friend: (Silence)

…Next week

Friend: "Dude, let's go to John's house, they have free booze all night!"

You: "I'm super tied up, I'm working on homework, you should come over, let's get some work done and watch a movie and eat ice cream."

…Friend never called again.

The moral of this example is that if you invite your "friends" to do meaningful productive things that you're into, they are most likely not going to follow through. Over time, people that are toxic or distracting will cut **themselves** off because they are not into the same things that you are into. See, you do not have to tell them you are cutting them off, simply don't feel obligated to do those things; rather, occupy yourself with things that make you HAPPY, FULFILLED, and PRODUCTIVE. Soon enough, you will come across people who enjoy the same things and you will be surrounded by powerful like-minded people!

Describe your **current** circle of friends:

_____

_____

_____

_____

_____

_____

_____

_____

_____

Describe your **ideal** circle of friends:

_____

_____

_____

_____

_____

_____

_____

_____

_____

Describe any **changes** that you need to make to have a stronger, supportive circle of friend:

_____
_____
_____
_____
_____
_____
_____
_____
_____
_____
_____
_____
_____
_____
_____
_____
_____
_____
_____
_____
_____
_____
_____
_____
_____
_____
_____
_____

Reflection Time

Take about 20 minutes, technology free and distraction free, to write how you envision your life to be moving forward once you have applied these changes to your circle.

_____
_____
_____
_____
_____
_____
_____
_____
_____
_____
_____
_____
_____
_____
_____
_____
_____
_____
_____
_____
_____
_____
_____
_____
_____
_____
_____
_____

Chapter 8

Turn Negatives into Positives

Do any of these comments sound familiar?

This world sucks.

I am bad at everything.

I hate my job, and my supervisor always has something against me.

I'm so fat.

I don't have any time.

I hate the way I talk

I feel that I am annoying

The president doesn't care about us; that is why I am struggling.

I am not smart enough.

My mom/dad doesn't love me.

I hate my hair.

I hate my skin.

I will never be successful because I do not know what I want to do.

My dad is a drug dealer, and my mom is an alcoholic, no one cares about my future.

I always get in trouble, why should I care.

I hate the color of my skin.

I have already disappointed everyone, what difference does it make?

I keep failing my tests; why should I care?

I failed that college class, I could never finish and get my degree.

I can't seem to do anything right in my life!

I have no friends.

I am always alone.

This world wouldn't even notice if I am gone. I hate my life; I am just going to ki...

Stop Right There!

Before the abundant amount of negative talk eats you alive and makes you feel worthless, please do me a favor. Understand that you ARE loved. You are amazing. You have an unlimited amount of opportunities coming your way. You are wanted! Did you see what just happened? A combination of negative self-talk and self-perception will indeed lead you to feel unworthy! Depending on how fragile your emotional state of mind is, this may lead to major depression and ultimately self-harm. This book will do no justice compared to hearing it directly from me, but here it goes: Don't ever think that no one loves you or cares about you because if you feel that no one out there does, I DO. I care about your wellbeing, I care about your success, and I care about your future, and I want you to be happy, fulfilled, and at peace.

It is easy to feel like a pebble in this world filled with bullies, mean people, unstable family members, and shady friends. We are in an enormous world with little to no "life and success guidance." I admit, this world is like Monopoly without instructions, and we have to do our best and treat ourselves the best to survive this thing called life. Most of your thoughts are self-appointed and self-validated, therefore; our thoughts become things, and as we think these negative thoughts, they become our reality.

For those that self-harm and feel like it is not worth even being here, remember what we talked about earlier, we are here for a reason and we have a purpose. Start having a purpose-driven life; and everything will follow. If you have an interest in animals, start looking into how you can make a career out of it or better yet, outside of your job or school, go volunteer and make some puppies happy! Pour your life into others in any way possible, and you will start to see your purpose unfold. Did you know that there are alternatives for when you are having these negative thoughts? Here are some of mine, if I ever feel down I:

- Bike ride in the city with headphones
- Listen to my favorite music
- Watch comedy videos
- Watch Ellen DeGeneres for some laughter
- Get inspired by Oprah
- Read a book to get my mind on a different path
- Watch Steve Harvey
- Hang out with my family, play with my nephew or chat with my mom about anything.
- Link up with Jenny, my best friend.
- Work out
- Eat buffalo chicken with ranch (this always makes me happy)
- Plan a getaway, even if it's to go hiking for the day

Listen to me; you need to be mentally healthy to recognize **when** you are spiraling out of control to **gain** control. Only you know your deep feelings and thoughts; therefore, you are the only one that can ultimately make a difference when it comes to the health of your mental state. When you do not take care of this critical aspect of your body, you may go into what's called a deep depression. Once a person is in a deep depression, professional help is advised to help untangle underlying emotions before complete control is lost. Make sure you are proactive about your mental health and the health of your overall body.

Develop A Solution-Based Mindset

One of the strongest skills I have developed and possess and enjoy teaching others to have is a solution-based mindset. Honestly, people always ask me how I am always so happy and energetic? How do I always keep pushing and never seem to be down? How do I stay focused on my goals regardless of what may happen? The answer is simple; I have a solution-based mindset that **turns negatives into positives.** That's right! I have developed an internal game plan that I follow faithfully day to day, regardless if I come across a random person yelling at me in the parking lot, or I didn't have a proposal approved for work that I worked so hard on for months. All it takes is for you to remain strong and become disciplined to go through the solution-based mindset process prior to breaking down or reacting toward a situation.

Solution-Based Mindset Breakdown

What does having a solution-based mindset really mean? **There is a solution to every problem!** Having a solution-based mindset means that when difficult or stressful situations occur you undergo a process to evaluate the scenario and create a game plan of solutions rather than focusing on the problem and remaining solution-less. Once you come up with your game plan, it's time to execute. Sometimes it may be difficult to tackle these tasks by yourself; it is recommended to include close family members, teachers, mentors or friends in this process. Many people may engage in a similar process already by calling their friends, venting, and asking for advice. The problem with just talking to a friend is that, often, it is not solution based. Ever asked for help from a friend and they either didn't know how to handle your situation, gave bad advice, or ignited the flame with more fire? We need to be careful of whom we allow to take advice from for our lives. There has to be structure, a positive one at that. When asking for advice refrain from turning it into a gossip get together; seek someone you trust and is level headed enough to provide positive direction. While developing this mindset, it is crucial to position yourself for success. In Chapter 4 we discussed the importance of believing in yourself, right? It is important to believe in yourself when tackling your life events.

The key principals in developing a solution-based mindset:

- Focus on brainstorming positive option(s) available
  - It is easy to get stuck dwelling on the actual problem, making it difficult to fathom that there are options available to solve the issue.
- Do not stay stuck on the past, focus on the future
  - Many times, it is easier to reminisce on the past and highlight insecurities to validate the impossibility of the solution. Focus on possibilities.

- Surround yourself with your support circle (lions and family)
  - o Reach out to your lions and positive family members to give you that extra support when you are feeling weak. There will be times that you will not have the strength to come up with solutions; this is the benefit of having people that love you to help you in this process.
- The problem is **not** the problem. (A problem *is simply the result of a situation*)
  - o This concept of "having a problem" kills any process in problem-solving. People that focus on the actual problem have already lost. When you focus on the issue, you are focusing on the past. The problem already happened, stop stressing over it and focus on what needs to happen next. Focus on the solution.
- Write it out – Map it out
  - o When brainstorming with lions or family members, we tend to talk for hours. Make sure that you take notes every time you think of solutions on your own or if you are discussing the situation with your support circle. People will give you great advice, and you will also come up with greats ideas, don't forget to write them down and prioritize them by effectiveness. Once you know it, you have developed a solution-based plan from A to Z. Congratulations!

- Believe in yourself
  - Facing problems head-on can be intimidating, but you need to believe that you are strong enough because you are! Repeat after me:
    - I dominate my situation, regardless of how hard it may get
    - I have the skills necessary to come up with the best solution
    - I will solve this and come out stronger
    - Nothing is too small or too big for me to handle
    - Lions and resources surround me, I will handle it well
    - I got this!

Reflection Time

Is there a situation or problem right now that you haven't been able to successfully work out?

According to the key principals discussed, how can you develop a solution-based mindset and get on the right path to solving your situation or problem?

_____
_____
_____
_____
_____
_____
_____
_____
_____
_____
_____
_____
_____
_____
_____
_____
_____
_____
_____
_____
_____
_____
_____

Chapter 9

Find A Mentor

H aving a mentor in your life is essential for your success, and this is a fact. All of my accomplishments are thanks to all of the mentors in my life who have helped me make great decisions, sort out ideas I have had for my future, or help me see the path in front of me as clear as can be overtime in life or business. Oprah Winfrey once said, "A mentor is someone who allows you to see the hope inside yourself. A mentor is someone who allows you to know that no matter how dark the night, in the morning joy will come. A mentor allows you to see the higher part of yourself when sometimes it becomes hidden to your own view." In this chapter, I will focus on the importance of finding a mentor and how it can benefit you and why having a mentor is a MUST.

Having a mentor is a must because they genuinely want to see you succeed. A mentor is like a friend that has the experience that you need and is willing to share their wisdom with you. Everyone has received advice, in one shape or another, from a mentor or an individual that changed their life or their mindset forever. A mentor is a dependable individual that shares excellent ideas with you and helps you create a plan and at times, connect you to the right people with strategic introductions.

Where It All Started

I have had several mentors throughout my life that have helped me navigate different areas of my life. My first mentor was Steve Kelley, he drilled my 8th-grade basketball team and I with discipline, life lessons, and ensured that we learned the value of hard work. Steve is an amazing man who takes the time to get to know a person, learns about their life goals, and best positions them for success. Steve was always intentional about educating me on career options according to what I was interested in and then discuss colleges that would be a great fit for me. These conversations I cherished the most because, aside from my mother and Raisa, another mentor of mine, Steve was an influential figure dedicated to my success. I will never forget him telling me that I had tremendous potential and that if I work hard and graduated college, he had no doubt in his mind that I would achieve anything that I put my mind towards. When he told me this, it was mind-blowing because I never had many individuals outside of my home talk to me about my future, and this sparked a flame of motivation that has never been extinguished!

I always knew that I could do well in the classroom, but I was never sure how my future would look. Hearing Steve tell me what he thought of me and my future motivated me to take his advice and chase my dream. Not only did we talk about school, colleges, and opportunities we also had conversations about life, friends, positive and negative habits, life consequences, even what I should be doing to prepare myself for future employment. These conversations opened up my mind to a world of possibilities outside of my inner-city home, and for that, I thank him forever. Steve was there throughout all of my decision making, such as repeating the eighth grade to apply to better schools, following through with going to my boarding high school regardless of my fears, along with my overall week-to-week teenage decision making. I am thankful for his willingness to be genuinely present, to love and to care for me throughout my life choices to ensure that I was well prepared. Having my father paralyzed and non-verbal due to suffering a stroke when I was a little girl, Steve truly watched over me, as a child of his. He was a key influence on the choices I have made throughout my adolescent years that instilled confidence in me. With all of that said, this was one of my inspirations in starting my Youth Leadership Organization, as I pay forward the mentorship to generations behind me.

As I developed into my teenage years and my college years, I organically connected with other mentors and advisors. Raisa Carrasco-Velez is another key mentor in my life who has developed into a life-long mentor! Raisa was another figure, back then, at the Boys and Girls Club of Lawrence whom I looked up to and received positive support. Raisa and I transitioned into a professional mentorship as I graduated from college and decided to start my own business. Raisa is currently a Youth Development Professional, and I had the privilege of having her as my professor throughout my master's program! I am so grateful to have someone so knowledgeable and so well connected in the community that genuinely cares about me and my mission—youth leadership development! Raisa and I occasionally meet up to catch up, and one thing I love doing is sharing all the fantastic things that I have going on within my business and professional world. I love the fact that she keeps me in check. As I give her a rundown of everything I have been up to and initiatives that are coming up - at the end of it - she always asks me; how are YOU doing? I appreciate that Raisa checks up on my self-care because she understands it is easy to get burnt out in this industry. Not many people stop and check in with their inner selves. People like Raisa are priceless, and I am overly humbled to have her on my support team.

Mentors For All Phases

I have had several other mentors who have played significant roles in my life as I developed into a young professional. This is a list of my mentors and what capacity they served so that you can have an idea of what types of people can be your mentor:

Mom: My number 1 supporter

Jenny Álvarez: Best friend, Business Partner/Mentor

Steve Kelley: Youth Basketball Coach, Mentor

Dr. Richard Lindsay: Mentor, RIP

Michelle Andrickson: Cousin, Mentor

Myra Ortiz: Friend, Mentor

Raisa Carrasco-Velez: Mentor, College Professor, Friend

Alejandra Young: High School Advisor, Friend, Mentor

Ron Hill: Business Mentor, Friend

Eduardo Crespo: Business Mentor, Friend

Tony Johnson: Former Co-Worker (Disney Internship), Friend, Mentor

Joan Kulash: Business Mentor

You can have a mentor for the **different areas** of your life as well. I currently have two business mentors that help me with business-related matters. There is no rule on how many mentors you have. Getting a mentor, for the most part, will happen organically and if you cannot seem to land a mentor, there are ways to get one intentionally.

How To Get A Mentor

Finding a mentor does not consist of any particular formula or step-by-step instruction. Mentorship happens organically. Most of the time, mentorship occurs without the official label of a mentor, and it takes place very casually. My basic rule of thumb is to observe those that you want to learn from. Do you know someone that is currently doing what you want to do in the future? Is there someone whom you admire because of their work ethic? Do you have a relationship with this person? If not, I highly recommend that you start being intentional by reaching out to this person. Communication can be via email, social media, or the next time you see them in person. When you establish the connection, assuming you have no relationship with this person, ask this person out for a cup of coffee and express to them your reason. Get personable, let them know what you like about them. Tell them what inspires you about their work and share your gratitude for their time. Mention that you have been interested in their job industry and you would like to learn more about it. If they are too busy to have a coffee, then have a quick phone chat. Afterward, send them a thank-you message, and ask if they would be willing to chat soon and possibly become a casual mentor. Once you received a yes, the relationship has begun. Of course, it will be more comfortable with people you already have a rapport with; however, if you have a relationship with the person, the process is the same.

It is important that you are coachable, listen, take advice, take criticism, respect the mentor's time by being on time, thank them often, and engage fully when in the actual conversations. Never make a mentor feel as though they are wasting their time or ever come across defensive; after all, mentorship is completely free; and most of the time they are doing this out of the kindness of their heart to pay it forward.

Reflection Time

Take about 20 minutes, technology free and distraction free, to write:

Who are youry mentors or who has the potential of being a mentor, and if I had a mentor, I would ask him or her the following questions:

_____
_____
_____
_____
_____
_____
_____
_____
_____
_____
_____
_____
_____
_____
_____
_____
_____
_____
_____
_____
_____
_____
_____
_____
_____
_____
_____

Chapter 10
The Truth About Failure

homas Jefferson once said, "Nothing can stop the man with the right mental attitude from achieving his goal; nothing on earth can help the man with the wrong mental attitude." It is evident that failure occurs every day, every month, and every year. It is impossible not to fail. My question is: what is your perception of failure? Many people view failure as the end of the world and ultimately breakdown for good. Ever heard a distraught person say, "I am such a failure, I can't do anything right!" This person's view on failure means that there are no other outlets once you have failed. It is okay to feel bad when you do not succeed; it is not okay to give up because of it.

The Secret

The truth is that failure is not the end of the world; it is merely an opportunity for you to realize that you need to try another way! That's it! Failure is very much like success. Once you achieve success, eventually, it's time to move on and continue making moves. Once you have failed, there will be a time to move on and continue making moves! If you can wrap your head around this concept, you will no longer look at failure as a final destination. Think about it this way, if you do not fail how do you know what works and what doesn't work? Over time, after I started running my business, I began to fall in love with the process, including failing. The reason why I looked forward to failing is that if I failed, I looked forward to learning from my mistakes. Aside from learning from my mistakes, I learned what worked and what didn't work. Lastly, when I failed, it allows me to brainstorm other ways to accomplish the current goal. Amusingly enough, when brainstorming, I come up with bigger and better ideas and I become ready to take on the next challenge. When I discovered this concept, boy was I unstoppable!

However; It Hurts

Failing is like running into a brick wall; it can hurt badly. For example, failing a test that you have been studying for or failing a certification that can lead to your next phase of success can be discouraging. However, you are still in control. If you get back up and apply some of the strategies that you have learned in previous chapters, such as making move S.O.L.O (strategically in order to land opportunities), you give yourself a chance to get back up, but this time stronger. Sometimes failing costs money, and once you have failed your confidence levels drop, pushing you to procrastinate your current task. It does stink, and it does not feel good. The good thing about failing so many times is that you end up growing a thick skin and becoming resilient toward complications that may occur in your life. It is the best thing that can happen to you! When we are emotionally soft and sensitive to things, it makes it difficult to get up and keep going. I identify myself as someone with tough skin however I have failed so many times and it still hurts; I am human. There have been times in my life when I have thought to myself, "Ahh forget it," yet I make a come back! I am so proud for not giving up! Had I given up, I would not be in the position I am in today: able to impact hundreds and thousands of lives and make a difference in my community and across the nation. Through good times and bad, what keeps me going is knowing that my story, my journey, and my philosophies have inspired others to get up and chase their best version of themselves, and this only motivates me to keep going for more. What drives you?

How To Change Your Mindset

1. **Shift your belief system around.** Failure is not a destination; it's more like a pit-stop. Keep exploring; keep learning!

2. **Keep growing.** Take every opportunity of failure as a moment to reflect, recharge, and re-execute.

3. **Brainstorm.** Use this moment to think about your next moves; it is important to self-evaluate and your next brainstorm maybe your biggest breakthrough.

4. **Seek help**. Remember we identified the importance of having a strong circle of friends? This is when you reach out and ask for help. We were not brought into this world alone, therefore you should not have to struggle and navigate life on your own.

5. **Motivate yourself.** Like I had mentioned in previous chapters, you need to watch what you say as you are your biggest cheerleader! It can be very fragile when you are at your lowest; pick yourself up and remember who you really are – Strong, resilient and capable!

Reflection Time

Take about 20 minutes, technology free and distraction free, to write: If you were not afraid to fail, what would you want to accomplish?

_____

_____

_____

_____

_____

_____

_____

_____

_____

_____

_____

_____

_____

_____

_____

_____

_____

_____

_____

_____

_____

_____

_____

_____

_____

_____

_____

_____

_____

_____

_____

_____

In closing...

I want every single person to understand that life is an unpredictable rollercoaster and only you have control over it. Many will read this book, get inspired in the moment and move on with their life without a tangible plan. Many will say that I accomplished my successes because I am special or smart, I'd beg to differ. I too had similar struggles to yours. I grew up in an inner city, I lost my father, I experienced peer pressure, I have been disrespected and experienced being bullied , I am also a first-generation student - the list goes on.

These adversities do not define you, they prepare you for whats to come. I am no different than you. I just tried, over and over again. If I did not understand something, I would ask until I did. I was curious. I wanted to be the best. I wanted success and I wasn't giving up. If I experienced failure, I reminded myself it was temporary and the next day will be a better day. Learn not to take life challenges too personally, instead learn how to best manage it and make the best of every situation.

Are you not happy? Ask yourself why. I constantly check in with myself and try hard to identify what is making me uneasy in order to tackle it head on. It may take some time to find the right answers, but don't give up. Personally, to help me dig deeper I list all of the possible reasons or things that may be bothering me. I then match my problems with possible solutions helping me prioritize the real areas of concern that need to be addressed. What is your process?

Please remember, I am no different than you. Do I have a bachelor's degree? Yes. Do I have a master's degree? Yes. Am I pursuing my Ph.D? Yes. However, I have accomplished these milestones because I put my mind to it and set my goals to complete it. Those were my personal goals, what are yours? I am no different than you, **believe me.**

CHEERS TO YOUR SUCCESS!

Let's Connect!

 @JoannaDePena

 /Bookjoannadepena

You Tube /JoannaDePena

∞ ∞ ∞

To Book Joanna de Pena for:

- **Motivational** Speaking Engagements
- **Facilitate** Educational Workshops & Trainings
- **Consulting** Administration & Organization
- **Coaching** Youth & Parents
- **Speaker** Conference Keynote

Email: info@joannadepena.com | **Website:** JoannaDepena.com

Made in the USA
Columbia, SC
02 March 2023

13196840R00057